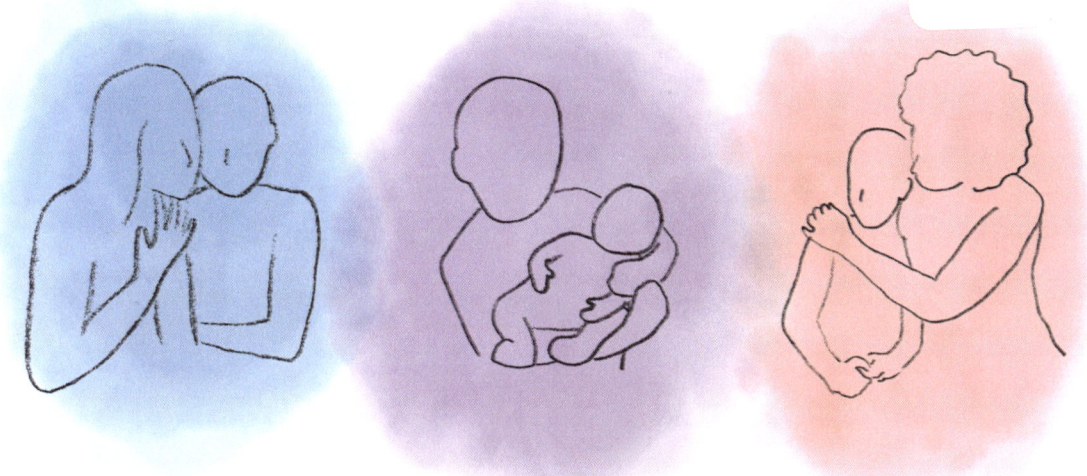

Let's Talk About Our Baby

A Book for Families After a Sudden Infant Death

 This book was commissioned by the Iowa SIDS Foundation to support all families after the loss of a baby, no matter the cause.

Written and Illustrated by
Laura Camerona, CCLS

www.wordsworthrepeating.com

Library of Congress Control Number: 2024940521

This book is intended to be read to a child by a trusted adult.

The advice and words within may not be suitable for every child or every situation.
It is suggested that the reader looks through the tips before reading this book with children.

The author would like to remind readers that after an unexpected loss,
the involvement of a mental health professional or support group is recommended.

This book is best suited for children ages 2-11.

ISBN Paperback: 979-8-9873529-7-7

www.wordsworthrepeating.com
Des Moines, Iowa

Tips for Reading This Book and Having Important Conversations with a Child:

- Follow the child's lead. If they aren't in the mood to read the book, save it for another moment.

- Stop and answer questions. If your child only wants to talk about one part of the book or one question that they have, it's okay to just focus on that.

- Bedtime isn't the best time for books about topics that kids may have questions about. It might lead to trouble sleeping. The first time you read this book with your child, try to avoid right before bedtime.

- The death of a baby is a very sad thing. It is okay if you cry when you read this book with your child. If your child seems concerned about your tears, explain that you are very sad that the baby died. This shows your child that it is okay to show sadness and talk about it.

- Don't expect a certain outword reaction from your child. It is okay if your child doesn't show the emotions that you might expect.

- Sometimes, kids grieve in waves. Sad and happy feelings might come and go rapidly.

- After you read this book with your child, remind them that they can talk about their baby or ask questions any time. Help your child list some people in their life that would feel comfortable talking about the baby and their death. Sometimes, kids choose adults who aren't their parents because they don't want to make their parent more sad.

- Kids may think about a death in new ways as they grow. If a child is young when a death happens, it may be appropriate to explain things or share this book with them as they get older.

- You aren't alone in this. The Iowa SIDS Foundation and other local SIDS Foundations provide support for families of any sudden unexpected infant death, no matter the cause.

- Check out the back of the book for more tips and specific phrases that can help support a child during this difficult time.

In memory of all babies gone too soon.
Always loved, always missed.

We had a baby.

Our baby was very special.

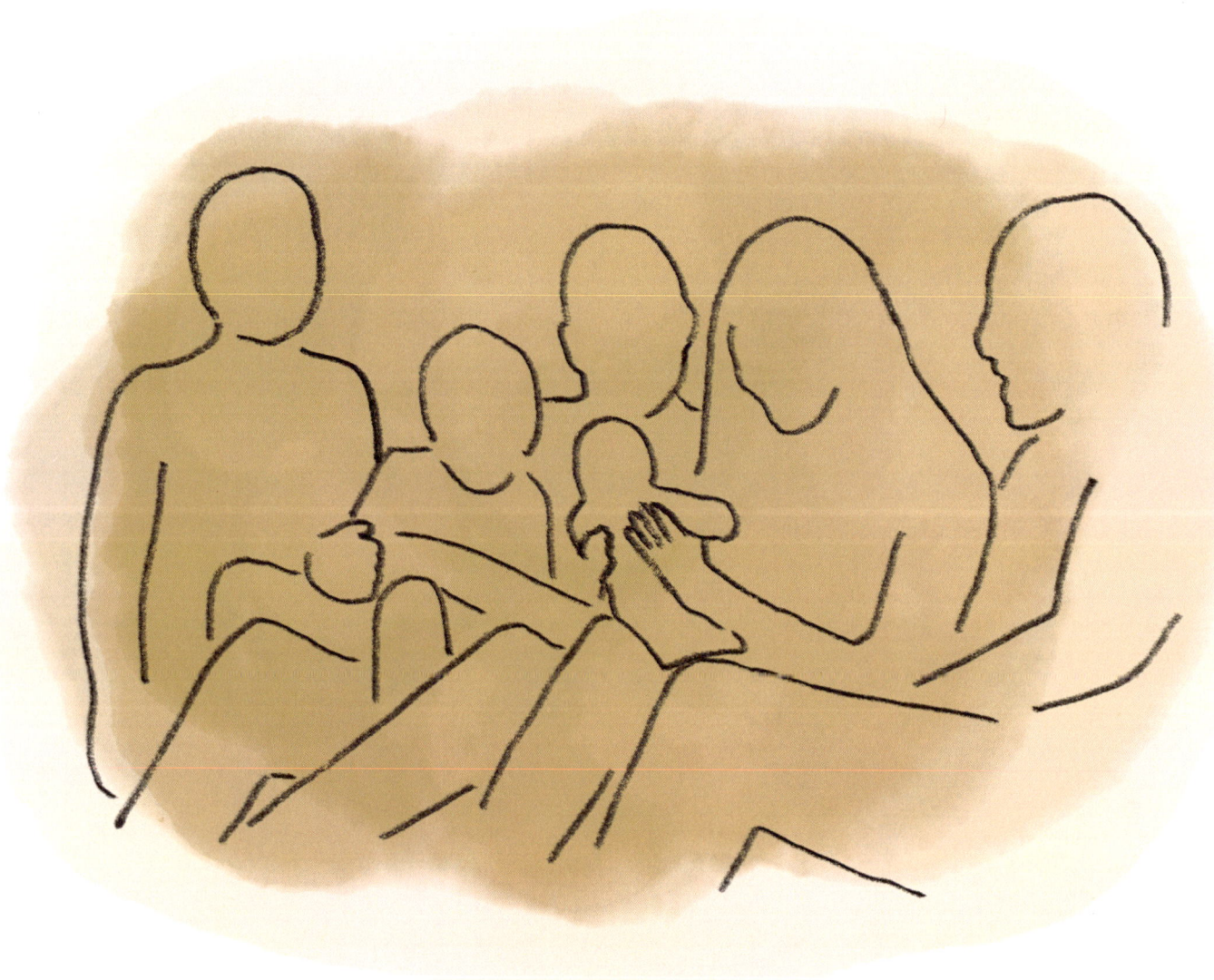

I liked holding our baby and
spending time together
as a family.

One day, something very sad happened.

Our baby died.

There was nothing that doctors could do
to help our baby live again.

Everyone is so sad
and surprised.
We had no idea that
this would happen.

We are not the only family
that this has happened to.

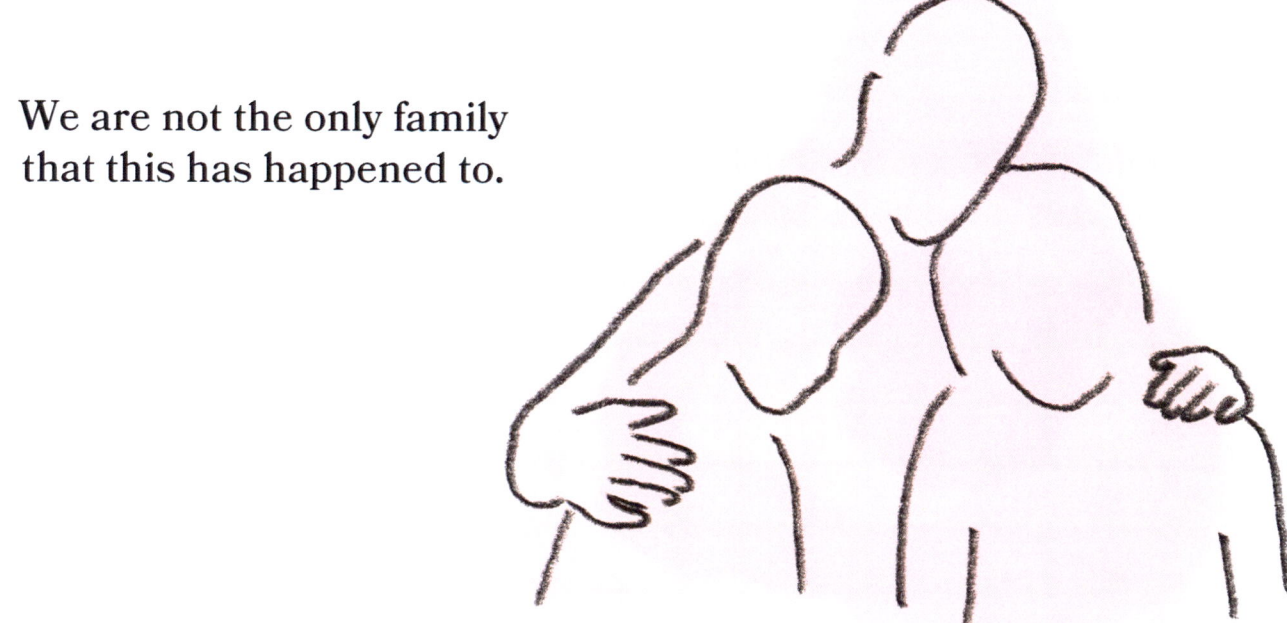

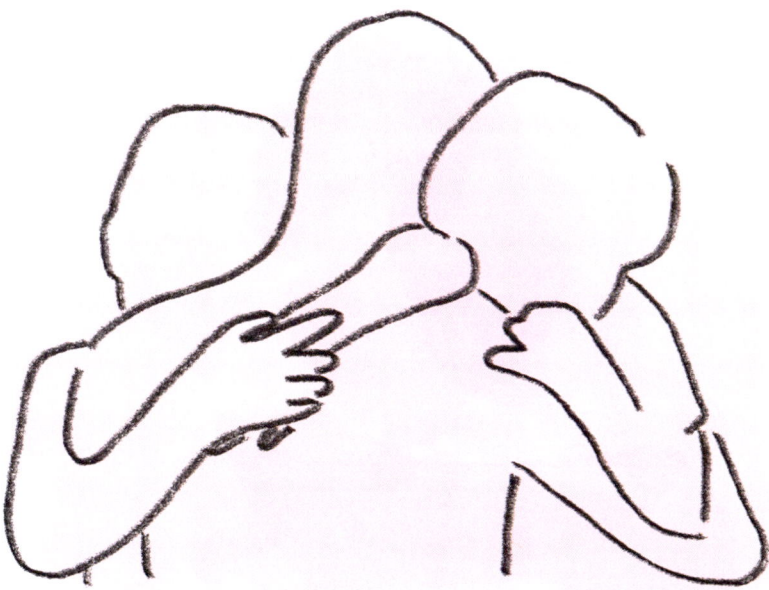

It doesn't happen very
often, but there are other
families that have had
babies die.

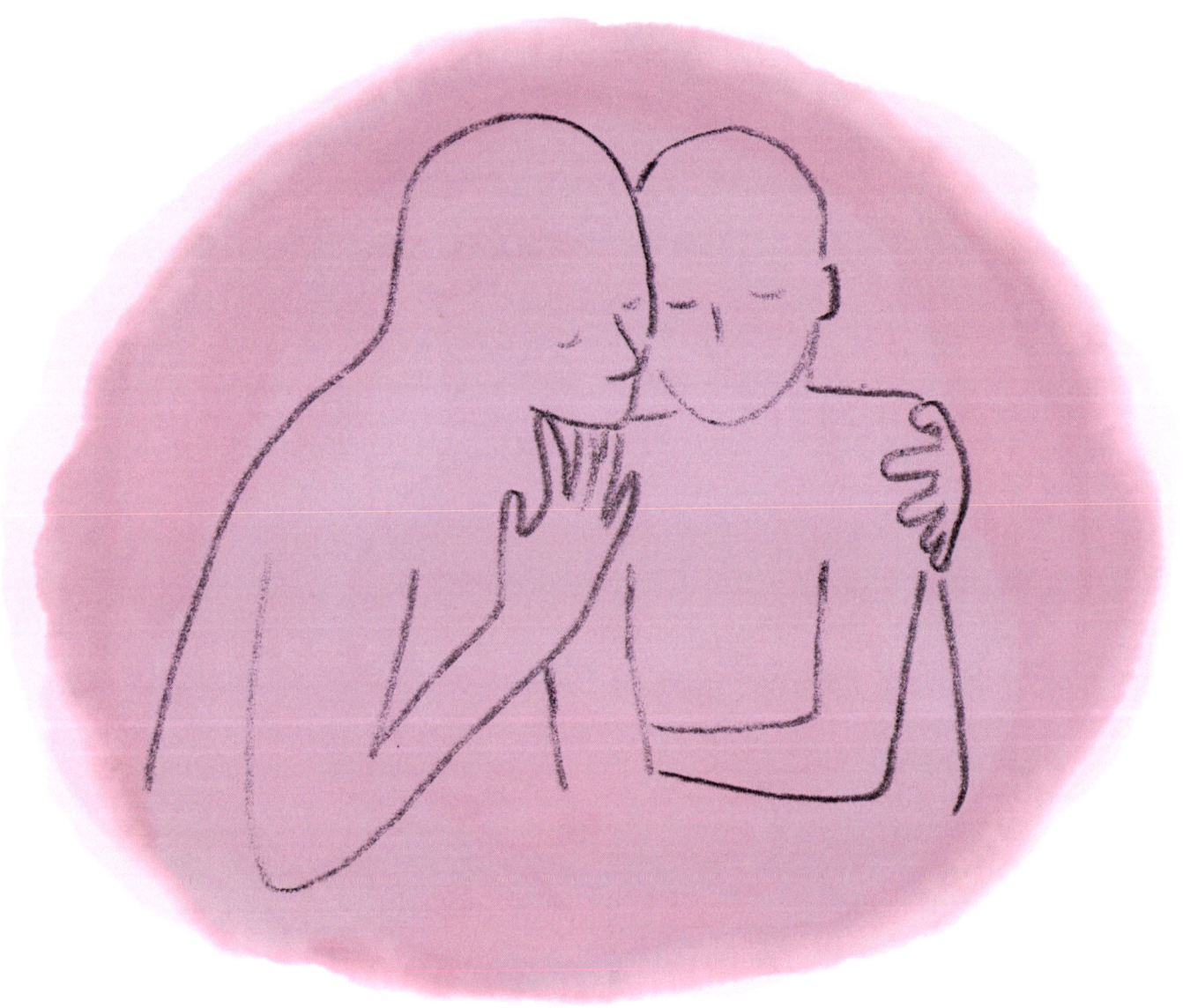

Sometimes, sad accidents happen.
Sometimes, no one can figure out why a baby died.

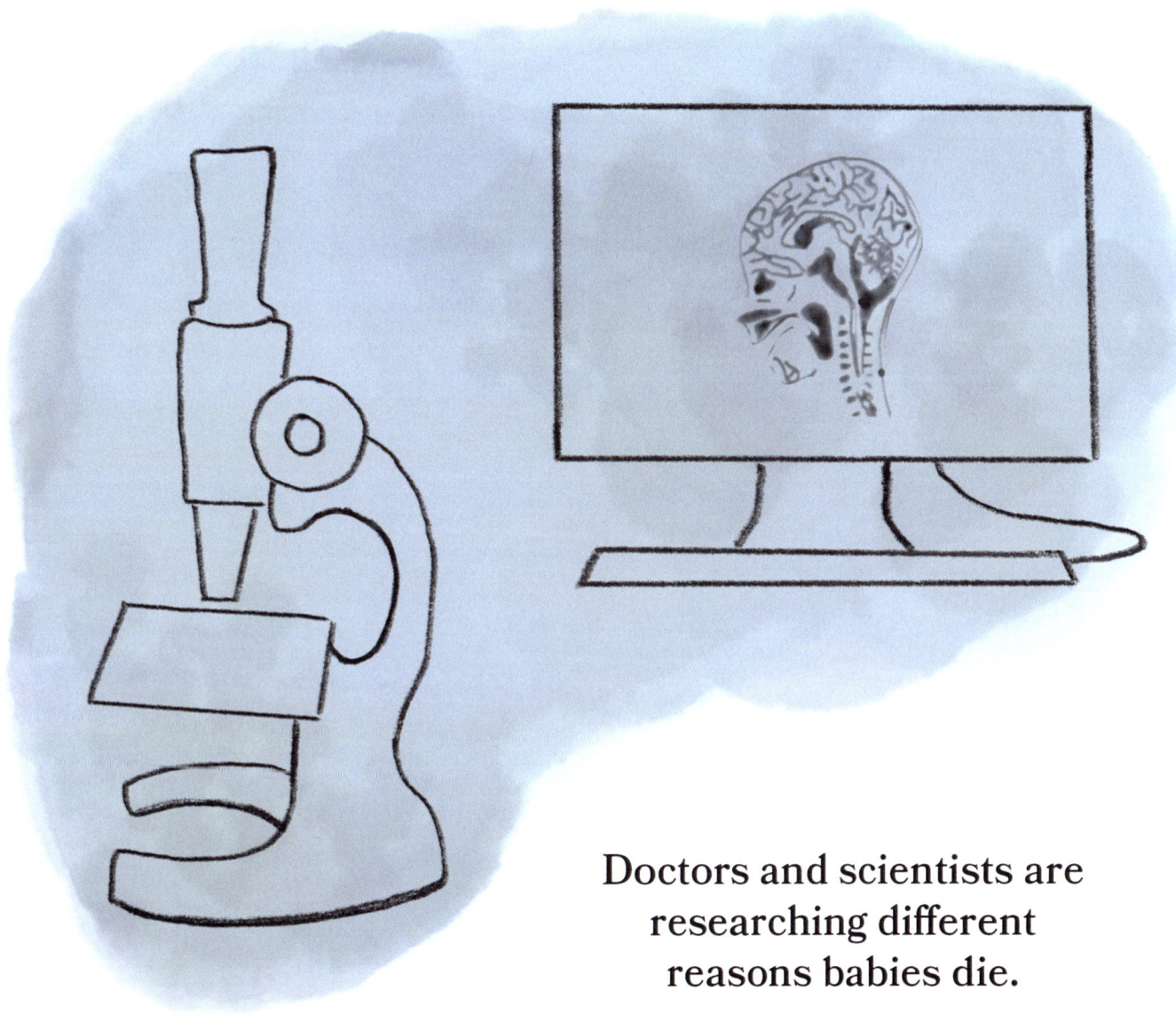

Doctors and scientists are researching different reasons babies die.

They want to do everything they can to keep babies safe.

No one wanted this to happen. Nothing you said
or did made this happen. Sometimes, sad things happen.

If a baby dies, the big sister or big brother is still a big sister or big brother. We will always be big brothers and big sisters.

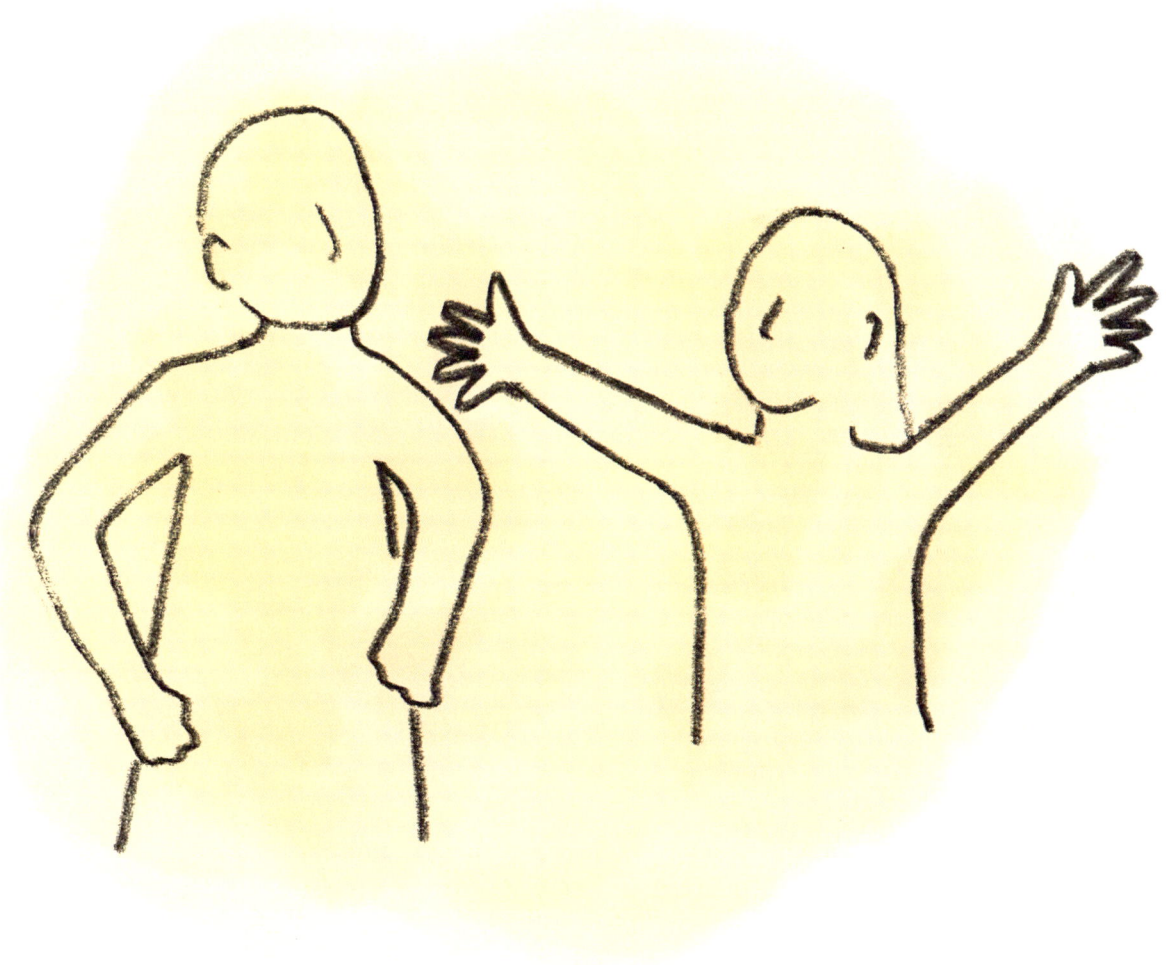

My whole family is sad.
We miss our baby.

Sometimes, I feel sad because I miss our baby. Other times,
I start thinking about other things, and I feel happy again.
This is okay. Whatever I feel is okay.

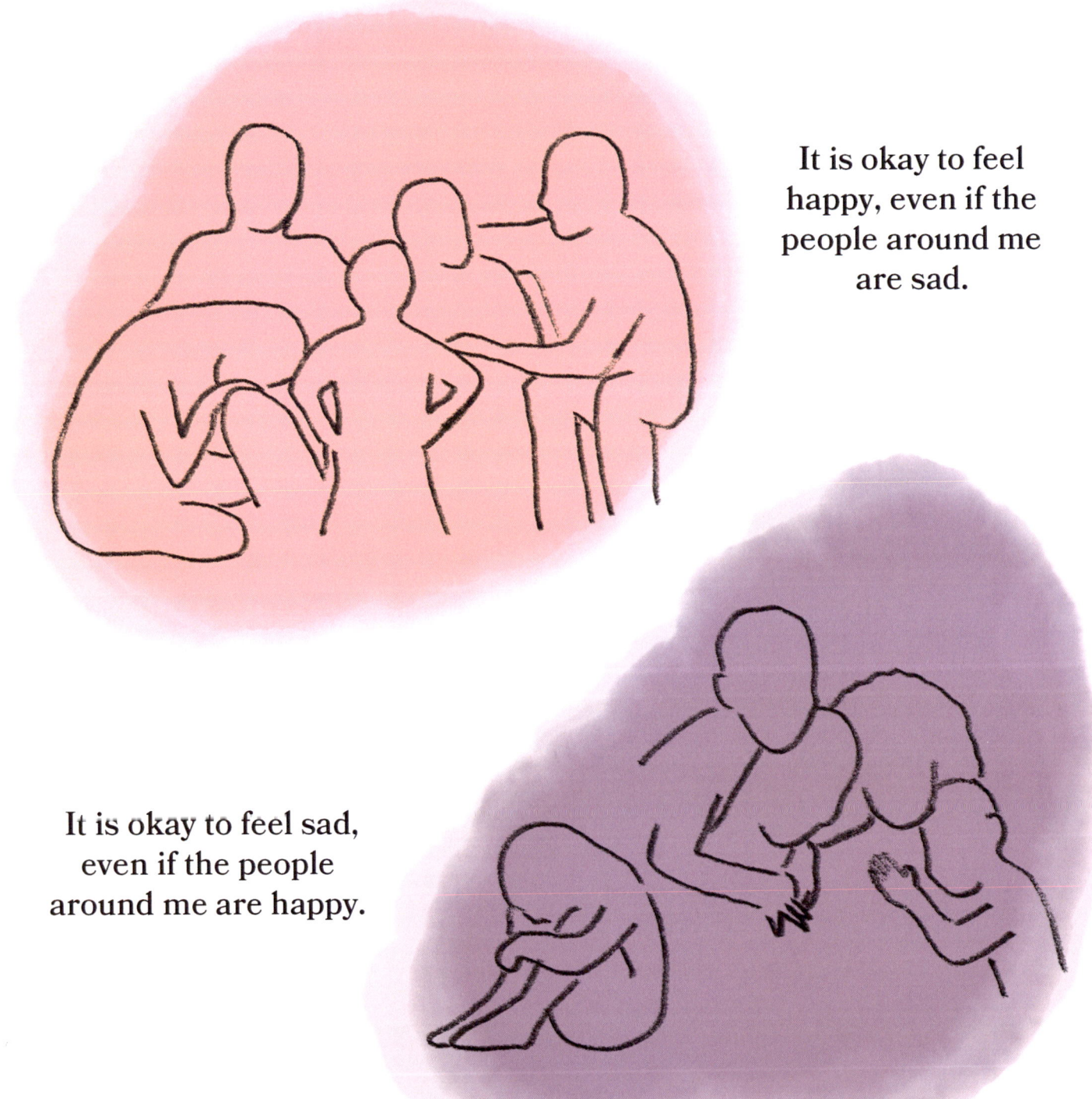

It is okay to feel happy, even if the people around me are sad.

It is okay to feel sad, even if the people around me are happy.

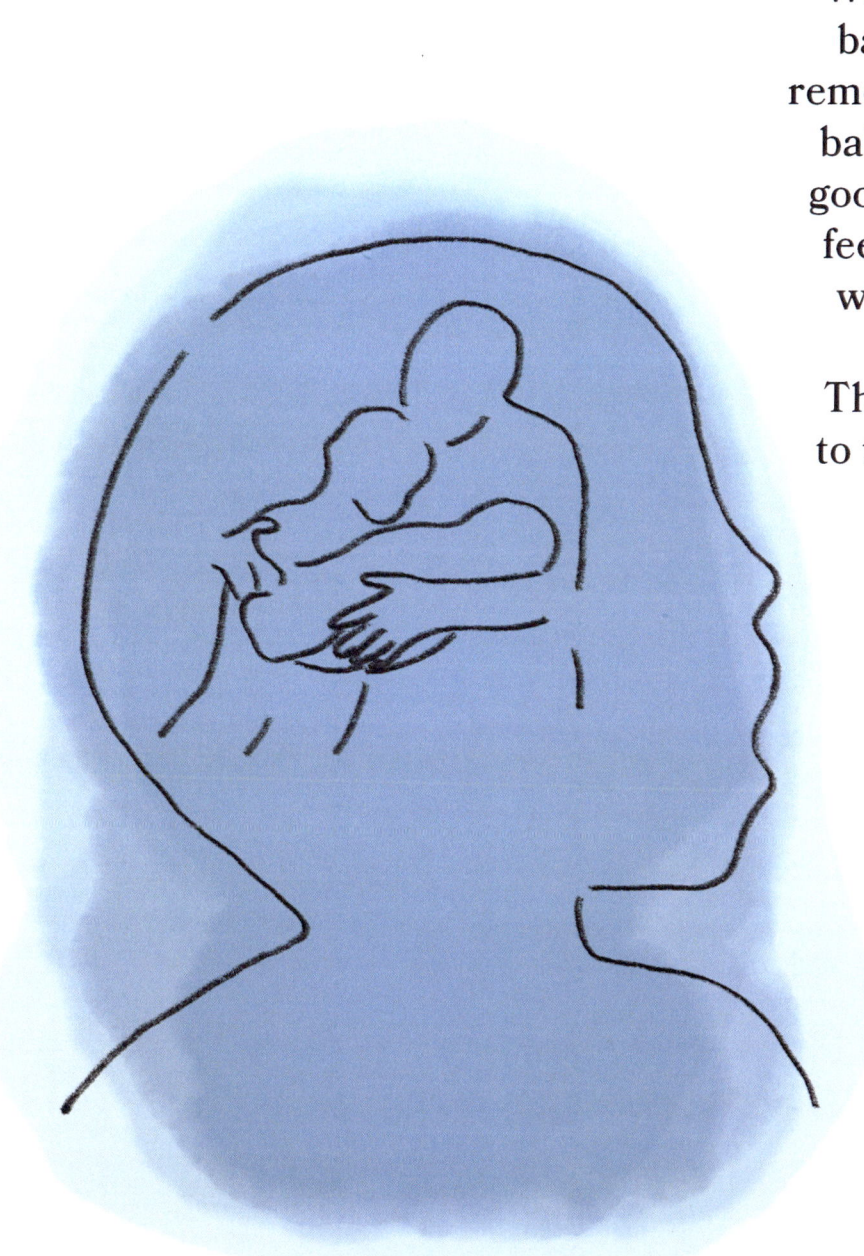

When I talk about our baby, it feels good to remember how sweet our baby was and to share good memories. It also feels sad to talk about when our baby died.

This is okay. It is okay to talk about our baby.

We can come up
with ways to
remember
our baby.

Our family can
write down our
memories,
look at pictures,
light a candle,
or create special
artwork.

Sometimes, I think about what life would be like if our baby was still alive. My family thinks about our baby too.

We will always remember our sweet baby. The memories of our baby will be a part of who we are and who we become.

Our baby will always be a part of our family.

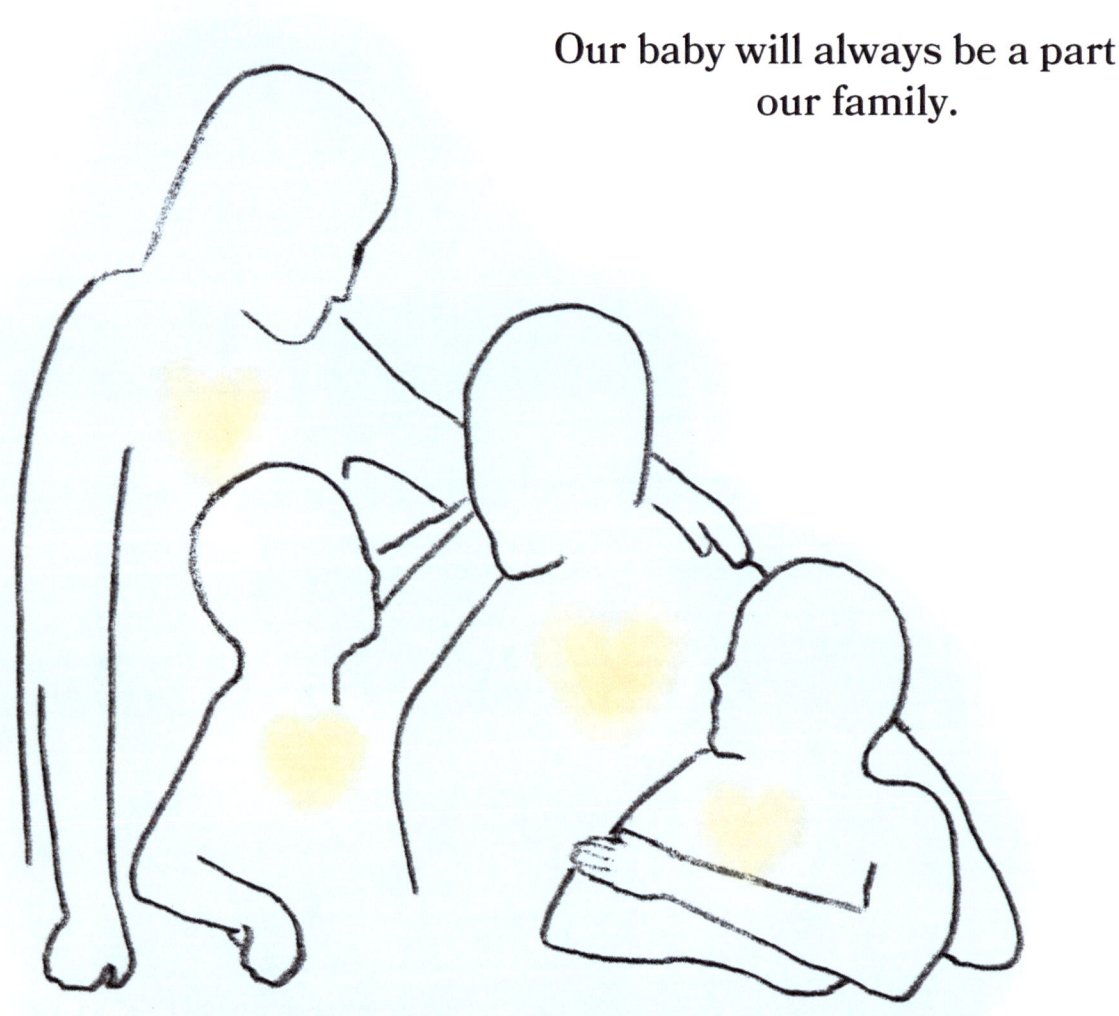

Remembering Our Baby

Our Baby's Name:

Our Baby's Birthday:

Our Baby weighed _____ **when they were born.**
Our Baby was _____ **inches long when they were born.**

The names of Our Baby's siblings are:

Our Baby looked so cute
when they wore:

Our Baby loved:
(ex. places to be, things/people to watch,
soothing activity...)

Our Baby's Picture

Special Projects Families Can Create Together
**When it feels right, doing one of these projects together can be a way for your family
to remember your baby and talk about feelings.**

Handprint/Footprint Project: If you have your baby's handprints or footprints,
you can use them or make copies of them to create these projects.

Family Tree: Create a family tree and use every person in the family's prints (hand or foot) as the leaves of a tree. This can be done on a canvas or digitally.

Butterflies: Have your child create a footprint butterfly and make one with the baby's footprints on the same canvas or paper.

Frame Art: Buy or repurpose a frame with wide and flat sides. Have your child decorate the frame however they wish. Display the baby's prints in this frame.

Special Place Project: Create a special place in your home/yard that reminds you of your baby.
Kids can help make one of these projects to display there.

Candle: Buy a clear glass from a thrift store. Have your child cut or tear tissue paper shapes. If they are older, they could cut it into hearts or the baby's name. Then have your child glue them to the outside of the glass with a school glue and water mixture (1 cup glue to 1/3 cup water). Have them coat the entire outside of the glass with the Mod Podge/glue mixture and add jewels if you desire. After the project dries, insert a candle into the glass. Find times as a family to light the candle and think or talk about your baby.

Garden Stone: Purchase a Garden Stone kit at your local craft store. Have your child help decorate the stone, and if you wish, add your baby's name to it. Place it in your yard or garden where you can visit it.

Tree/Flower: As a family, plant a flower or tree in memory of your baby.

Jewelry Project: Each family member can create one of these projects to wear
or to keep close on days that they want to feel close to their baby.

Family Necklace/Bracelet: Provide your child a variety of beads and a string. Have your child choose a bead for each family member. The bead could be symbolic based on color, shape, anything! If they don't do it on their own, ask if they would like to include a bead for the baby. If they chose not to, that is okay. You can talk about what a great team your family is during this project and how strong your love is.

Paper Beads: Better activity for older children. Provide scrapbook paper. Have the child chose paper that is special to them. Have them cut a long thin triange (approximately 3/4 in wide and 9 in long). On the white side, have them write a message to themselves, the baby's name, anything! Starting on the wide end wind the paper tightly, so that the message on the inside of the bead and the colorful side is out. Rolling it with a pencil or straw can be helpful. Seal with school glue/water mix (1 cup glue/1/3 cup water).

Special Day Project: Create something that you might not see every day, but that
you might pull out every so often or on a special holiday to remember your baby.

Holiday Ornament: Find a simple flat ornament or a ball and add the baby's name to it. Allow your child to decorate. Many parents choose to also make one themselves.

Blank Book/ScrapBook: Use a blank book or journal. Fill the pages with family memories of being pregnant, photos, pictures your child draws, written out feelings, anything. Get the book out on days when your family wants to spend more time remembering your baby.

Ideas for Explaining Hard Things and Answering Kids Questions

After the loss of a baby, adults are experiencing so many hard thoughts and feelings. Trying to support a young child after a sudden death can be overwhelming. Here are some things you can try to remember:

Kids benefit from routine. It helps them know what to expect and makes them feel safe. Do what you can to keep your other children's routines the same. If they are old enough, talk to them about what they do or don't want to do in the weeks after the death.

Be honest, but keep things simple. Kids talk to other kids, and kids listen to adult conversations. By telling a child the truth and answering their questions in a simple way, you can keep their trust.

Avoid placing blame on another person that your child is close to. If you believe the death of your baby was the fault of someone else, try to minimize those conversations with a child. In the days ahead, there might be court cases and trials, and it is ideal to leave your child out of all of that as much as possible.

It can be overwhelming to try to explain the death of a baby to a child. Here are some simple, but honest phrases that might help depending on the cause of your baby's death.

"We don't know exactly what happened, but there are a lot of people that are trying to figure it out."

"When babies are very young, they can't always move their heads when their breathing gets blocked. No one knew that our baby couldn't breathe. So we didn't know the baby needed help."

"_____ made a mistake. They didn't know that the baby was going to get hurt."

"The doctors say that there was a part of the baby's body that wasn't working right. The baby was born like that, but we didn't know."

"The doctors and nurses were doing everything they could to help our baby, but the baby got too sick. To stay alive, a person's _____ (brain/heart/essential organ) has to work. Our baby's _____ (same organ) wasn't working anymore."

Please consider contacting a mental health professional to help you support you and your child through the hard days ahead.

FB: @IowaSIDSFoundation
Instagram: @iowasids
LinkedIn: Iowa SIDS Foundation

This book was commissioned by the Iowa SIDS Foundation in celebration of their 20th Anniversary. Since 2004, the Iowa SIDS Foundation has been dedicated to supporting Iowa families, empowering professionals, and saving babies. With the belief that even one infant loss is too many, the Iowa SIDS Foundation is passionate about helping all babies reach their first birthday and beyond. To find more and support our mission, visit us at www.iowasids.org.

Laura Camerona, CCLS worked as hospital Child Life Specialist for 15 years. During this career, Laura wished for books that gave families the right words to talk about important things. Laura started Words Worth Repeating and now spends her time partncring with families and with non-profit organizations to create unique children's books that help families have important supportive conversations about topics and events that have an effect on their lives. Follow her work and find more of her books on her website and socials.

www.wordsworthrepeating.com

FB: @WordsWorthRepeatingBooks
Instagram: @words.worth.repeating
LinkedIn: Words Worth Repeating